S0-ADF-675

JACKSONVILLE
JAGUARS

by Matt Tustison

Published by ABDO Publishing Company, 8000 West 78th Street, Edina, Minnesota 55439. Copyright © 2011 by Abdo Consulting Group, Inc. International copyrights reserved in all countries. No part of this book may be reproduced in any form without written permission from the publisher. SportsZone™ is a trademark and logo of ABDO Publishing Company.

Printed in the United States of America,
North Mankato, Minnesota
062010
092010

 THIS BOOK CONTAINS AT LEAST 10% RECYCLED MATERIALS.

Editor: Chrös McDougall
Copy Editor: Nicholas Cafarelli
Interior Design and Production: Christa Schneider
Cover Design: Christa Schneider

Photo Credits: Steven Cannon/AP Images, cover; Michael S. Green/AP Images, 1, 4, 7, 8, 42 (middle); Bryan Kelsen/AP Images, 10; Rick Wilson/AP Images, 12, 15, 31, 37, 42 (top), 43 (middle), 47; Phil Long/AP Images, 17; David J. Phillip/AP Images, 18; David Stluka/AP Images, 20; Al Behrman/AP Images, 22, middle (bottom); Chuck Burton/AP Images, 24; Don Frazier/AP Images, 26, 43 (top); Tony Gutierrez/AP Images, 29; Paul Spinelli/AP Images, 33; John Russell/AP Images, 34; Stephen Morton/AP Images, 39 43 (bottom); Phil Coale/AP Images, 40; Mark Duncan/AP Images, 44

Library of Congress Cataloging-in-Publication Data
Tustison, Matt, 1978-
  Jacksonville Jaguars / Matt Tustison.
      p. cm. — (Inside the NFL)
  Includes index.
  ISBN 978-1-61714-015-0
  1. Jacksonville Jaguars (Football team)—History—Juvenile literature. I. Title.
  GV956.J33T87 2011
  796.332'640975912—dc22
                              2010014964

TABLE OF CONTENTS

CHAPTER 1

MILE HIGH SURPRISE

The Jacksonville Jaguars were playing in only their second season in the National Football League (NFL). They found themselves in an amazing, unlikely situation.

The Jaguars were leading the Denver Broncos 23–12 in the fourth quarter of a second-round playoff game on January 4, 1997. The crowd of 75,678 at Mile High Stadium in Denver was stunned silent. Their beloved Broncos had been favored to win the game by two touchdowns.

The Jaguars were an expansion team. That meant they had been new the previous season.

In NFL history, no expansion team had played this well so quickly. Usually it took expansion teams many years before they could compete with the NFL's best squads.

Jacksonville's team was made up mostly of players whom other NFL franchises did not want. Head coach Tom Coughlin had no experience in that job except at the college level.

KEENAN MCCARDELL CELEBRATES AFTER CATCHING A TOUCHDOWN PASS IN THE THIRD QUARTER AGAINST DENVER IN THE 1997 PLAYOFFS.

SURPRISE SUCCESS

Jacksonville went 4–12 in 1995. The Carolina Panthers also made their NFL debut that year. They finished 7–9. Previously, no NFL expansion team had won more than three games in its first season. The last time the NFL had added expansion teams was in 1976. The Tampa Bay Buccaneers finished 0–14 during that first season while the Seattle Seahawks were 2–12. The Jaguars and Panthers both reached a conference championship game in their second seasons.

That success was partly due to free agency. A free agent is a player who has completed his contract and is free to sign with any team. Free agency fully started in the NFL in 1993. Before then, far fewer players switched teams. Jacksonville, for example, signed wide receiver Keenan McCardell after he had enjoyed some success with the Cleveland Browns. Once he was with the Jaguars, he became an even better player.

Almost no one thought the Jaguars could win. Woody Paige, a columnist for the *Denver Post,* had written in that morning's newspaper, "Can we get a legitimate [real] team in here next Sunday?" He and many others assumed that the Broncos would easily advance to the following week's American Football Conference (AFC) Championship Game.

But the Jaguars, behind quarterback Mark Brunell's clever passing and scrambling and Natrone Means' powerful but nimble running, had taken that 11-point lead. There were about 10 minutes left in the game. If the Jaguars could hold on, it would be one of the NFL's most shocking moments ever.

JAGUARS QUARTERBACK MARK BRUNELL SEARCHES FOR AN OPEN RECEIVER AGAINST DENVER IN THE 1997 NFL PLAYOFFS.

JAGUARS DEFENSIVE END TONY BRACKENS TAKES DOWN BRONCOS QUARTERBACK JOHN ELWAY DURING JACKSONVILLE'S 30–27 WIN.

Denver was not going to make it easy, though. The Broncos had star quarterback John Elway on their side, as well as many other talented offensive players. One of them, Terrell Davis, scored on a 2-yard touchdown run. He then ran in a two-point conversion. The score became much closer, 23–20 in the Jaguars' favor.

The pressure was back on Jacksonville. Mile High Stadium was one of the noisiest venues in the NFL. How would the Jaguars handle this difficult situation?

Very well, it turned out. Brunell led the Jaguars 74 yards down the field in nine plays. On one of them, he scrambled for a 29-yard gain by dodging four Broncos. He finished the drive with a 16-yard touchdown pass to Jimmy Smith. "All I had to do was hold my arms out," Smith said of the pass in the corner of the end zone that went just out of a defender's reach. "It was perfect." Jacksonville took a 30–20 lead with 3:39 left.

Denver scored a late touchdown, but it was not enough. Jacksonville had done what many thought was impossible. The Jaguars, in just their second season, had beaten the powerful Broncos 30–27. In the regular season, Denver had gone 13–3, tied for the best record in the NFL. Jacksonville had to win its final five games just to reach 9–7 and sneak into the playoffs.

"I'm sick to my stomach," Davis said after the game.

The Broncos wanted to get to the Super Bowl for Elway, whose career was nearing the end. The Jaguars were hungry, too. Many of their players had been let go by other NFL teams. They were determined to show that those teams had made mistakes. They proved that against the Broncos.

JACKSONVILLE RECEIVER KEENAN MCCARDELL HAULS IN A 31-YARD
TOUCHDOWN PASS IN THE 1997 PLAYOFF GAME AGAINST DENVER.

SIMPLY THE BEST?

Are the Jaguars the top expansion team in NFL history? In terms of immediate success, the answer is yes. Jacksonville qualified for the playoffs in four of its first five seasons. No other NFL expansion team has accomplished that feat.

"People don't believe we're supposed to be here," said wide receiver Keenan McCardell, who had struggled before signing with Jacksonville in 1996. "But, hey, it don't matter, it don't matter."

Thanks to smart decisions in selecting coaches and players, the Jaguars had become a good team surprisingly fast. Amazingly, the next week Jacksonville found itself one step away from reaching the Super Bowl. It was not to be, however. The Jaguars lost 20–6 to the host New England Patriots in the AFC Championship Game.

The Jaguars, though, had proven that expansion teams did not need to wait long to compete with the NFL's best teams. In fact, Jacksonville would go on to reach the playoffs in the next three seasons, too. The team would also make the AFC Championship Game a second time after the 1999 season. The Jags fell short in that game, as well, losing 33–14 to the Tennessee Titans.

The Jaguars started very strongly in their first five seasons, but since then they have not won consistently. They have discovered, like many teams before them, that succeeding in the playoffs and reaching professional football's biggest game—the Super Bowl—is not easy.

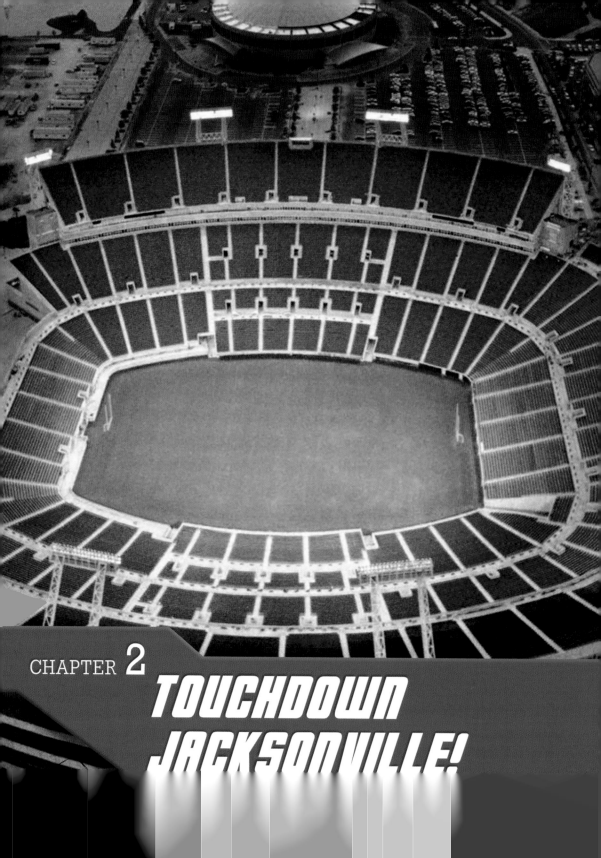

CHAPTER 2

TOUCHDOWN JACKSONVILLE!

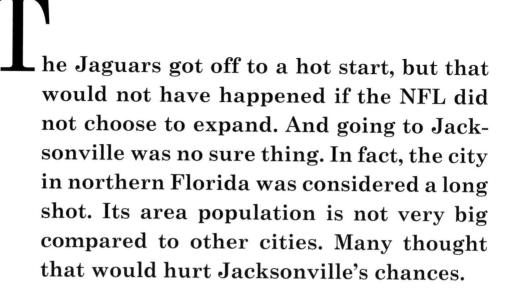

The Jaguars got off to a hot start, but that would not have happened if the NFL did not choose to expand. And going to Jacksonville was no sure thing. In fact, the city in northern Florida was considered a long shot. Its area population is not very big compared to other cities. Many thought that would hurt Jacksonville's chances.

Jacksonville's attempt to get an NFL team began on August 17, 1989. That was when the Touchdown Jacksonville! business partnership was formed. On September 16, 1991, Touchdown Jacksonville! filed an expansion application with the NFL. The application listed a nine-member group that included J. Wayne Weaver. He later would become the main owner of the Jaguars.

The NFL announced in March 1992 that it planned to add two expansion teams. In May 1992, Jacksonville made the NFL's list of five finalists. The other finalists were:

THE GATOR BOWL WAS FIXED UP AND NAMED MUNICIPAL STADIUM BEFORE THE JAGUARS' NFL DEBUT IN 1995.

Baltimore, Maryland; Charlotte, North Carolina; Memphis, Tennessee; and St. Louis, Missouri. Baltimore and St. Louis had hosted NFL teams before, but the teams' owners had moved them to other cities.

Touchdown Jacksonville! had received a commitment of $60 million from the Jacksonville City Council to fix up the Gator Bowl, the city's largest football stadium. In 1993, the NFL informed Touchdown Jacksonville! that additional renovations would be needed. At first, a solution could not be reached. However, eventually a new plan was agreed upon. The city would provide $53 million for renovations, and $68 million would come from team sources.

On October 26, 1993, the NFL announced that the existing team owners had unanimously voted for Charlotte to receive the league's twenty-ninth team. That team became known as the Carolina Panthers. That left one more expansion team to be awarded. On November 30, 1993, it became official: The Jacksonville Jaguars were named the league's thirtieth team. They would join the Panthers as new NFL teams in 1995.

On December 1, 1993, the *Florida Times-Union*, Jacksonville's daily newspaper, ran a

FOOTING THE BILL

J. Wayne Weaver was able to become the Jaguars' main owner because he had made a lot of money in the shoe business. After high school, the Georgia native began a series of jobs at Brown Group, a clothing company based in St. Louis, Missouri. In 1978, he left to start his own shoe company, Nine West, which specialized in women's footwear. Weaver eventually also became the operator of another footwear company, Shoe Carnival. After his partnership group was awarded the Jaguars, Weaver and his wife, Delores, moved from Connecticut to Jacksonville.

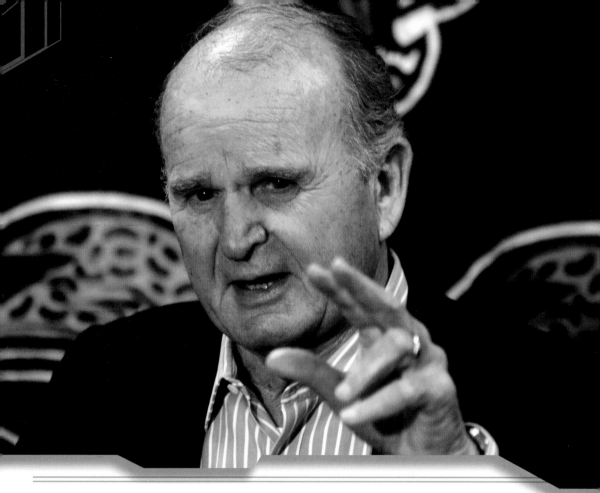

J. WAYNE WEAVER, SHOWN IN 2010, HAS BEEN THE JAGUARS' PRIMARY OWNER FROM THE START.

front-page headline in huge type. It read, "DO YOU BELIEVE IN MIRACLES? YES." That evening, approximately 25,000 fans celebrated at the Gator Bowl as season-ticket sales began. Within two weeks, the Jaguars had already sold more than 55,000 seats.

Clearly, Jacksonville was ready for some football. Now the Jaguars organization needed to get started on the hard work of building a team from scratch. A successful businessman, Weaver wanted a model football team and one that would contend for the playoffs fast.

One of Weaver's key moves was hiring Tom Coughlin as Jacksonville's coach and director of football operations in February 1994. That decision came 19 months before the Jaguars' first game. Coughlin had been a successful head coach at Boston College but had no experience as an NFL head coach. However, he had served under the New York Giants' Bill Parcells as wide receivers coach from 1988 to 1990. Coughlin, like his mentor, stressed discipline. He also was good at planning, and in Jacksonville he had time to do so.

Another step for the Jaguars in building their team took place at the NFL Expansion Draft on February 15, 1995. The two new teams, the Jaguars and Panthers, took turns making picks from existing NFL teams. The Jaguars had the first pick and selected quarterback Steve Beuerlein. Jacksonville chose 31 players in all. A few, including Beuerlein, linebacker Keith Goganious, wide receiver Willie Jackson, offensive guard Jeff Novak, became starters.

Probably even more important to Jacksonville was the 1995 NFL Draft, held on April 22–23 in New York. The Jaguars selected mammoth offensive tackle Tony Boselli, a former University of Southern California standout, with the number two pick.

SECOND CHANCES

Jimmy Smith overcame obstacles early in his career. Smith broke his leg and missed most of his rookie season with the Dallas Cowboys in 1992. The next year, he needed an emergency operation to remove his appendix. He also suffered through infection and stomach problems. He did not play in 1994 after being released by Dallas and Philadelphia. In 1995, he earned a tryout with the Jaguars after his mother sent head coach Tom Coughlin a binder filled with newspaper articles. He became a five-time Pro Bowl selection with the Jaguars.

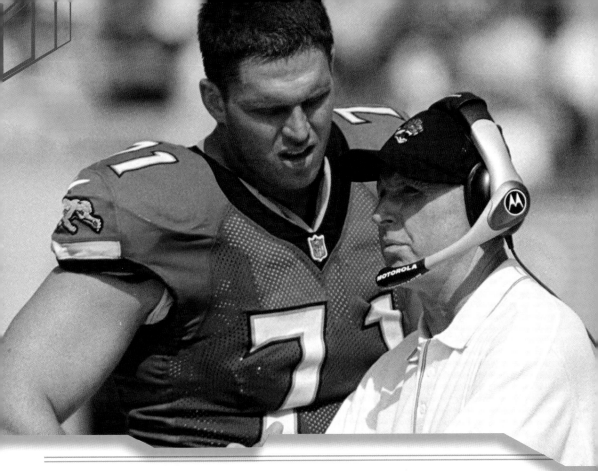

TONY BOSELLI (71) TALKS TO COACH TOM COUGHLIN IN 2000. BOSELLI WAS SELECTED FOR FIVE PRO BOWLS DURING SEVEN YEARS WITH THE TEAM.

Boselli would be selected to five Pro Bowl teams.

Jacksonville did not just rely on the drafts. In February 1995, the team had signed wide receiver Jimmy Smith, who had been out of the NFL in 1994. Also, on April 21, 1995, the day before the NFL Draft, the Jaguars traded the rights to their third- and fifth-round picks to the Packers for quarterback Mark Brunell.

Through a variety of ways, Coughlin had built a roster with many talented players. The Jaguars were now prepared for their debut season. Ready, set, hike!

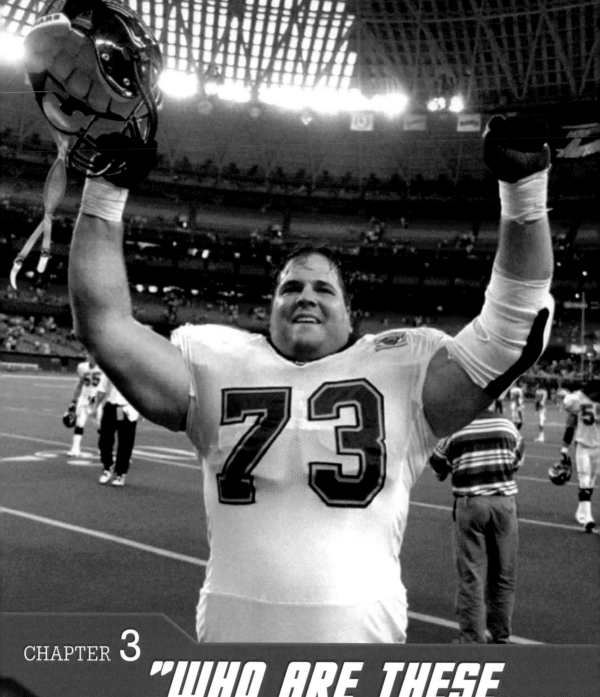

CHAPTER 3

"WHO ARE THESE GUYS?"

O n September 3, 1995, the Jaguars played their first-ever regular-season game at Jacksonville Municipal Stadium—the new name of the Gator Bowl stadium that had been almost completely fixed up. In front of a crowd of 72,363, the Jaguars lost to the Houston Oilers 10–3.

The Jaguars had built a talented roster, but the team was young and inexperienced. It finished 4–12 in its first season. Still, many of the losses were close. Also, the Jaguars made an important discovery when Brunell took over for Beuerlein as the starting quarterback and excelled. In Green Bay, Brunell had been stuck on the bench behind star Brett Favre. But now as a Jaguar, he finally had the opportunity to perform.

FRANCHISE FIRSTS

The Jaguars' first-ever regular-season win came in their fifth game. They defeated the Oilers 17–16 in Houston on October 1, 1995. The next week, Jacksonville beat eventual AFC champion Pittsburgh 20–16 for the first home win. The Jaguars' other two victories in 1995 came against the Cleveland Browns.

BRIAN DEMARCO CELEBRATES JACKSONVILLE'S FIRST WIN. IT WAS A 17–16 VICTORY OVER THE HOUSTON OILERS ON OCTOBER 1, 1995.

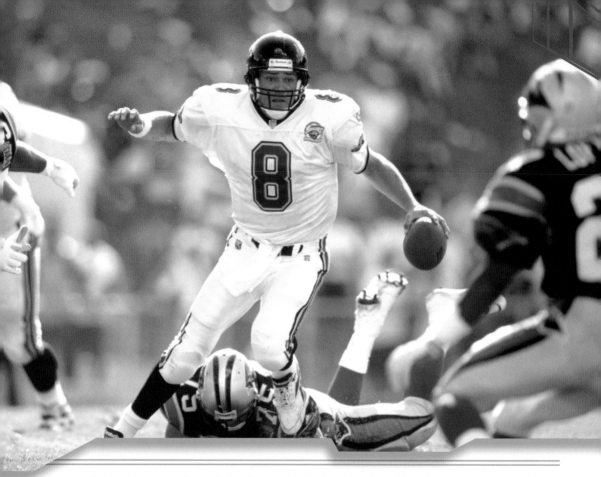

MARK BRUNELL AND THE JAGUARS LOST TO FELLOW EXPANSION TEAM CAROLINA DURING A 1995 PRESEASON GAME.

Coughlin added more talent before the Jaguars' second season. The team signed running back Natrone Means and wide receiver Keenan McCardell. Jacksonville also added some key players on defense. In the 1996 NFL Draft, the Jaguars took linebacker Kevin Hardy, defensive end Tony Brackens, and cornerback Aaron Beasley.

Jacksonville entered the 1996 season looking to build off its promising first year. The Jaguars got off to a shaky start, though, at 4–7. The turning point was a game on November 24 in Baltimore against the Ravens.

Jacksonville trailed 25–10 in the fourth quarter. A loss would have meant that the Jaguars almost certainly would not make the playoffs. They did not quit, though. The Jaguars rallied to tie the score on two touchdown passes by Brunell. Then, in overtime, Mike Hollis' 34-yard field goal gave Jacksonville a 28–25 win.

That victory demonstrated that the Jaguars were fighters. Jacksonville went on to win its final four regular-season games, too. Then the Jaguars made a remarkable playoff run, with victories at heavily favored Buffalo and Denver. Only in its second season in the NFL, the team got within one win of reaching the Super Bowl.

"I think the lack of respect is obvious," Brunell said a few days after the Jaguars' upset of the Broncos. "It's like, 'Who are

KINDER, GENTLER

Jaguars coach Tom Coughlin was known for being strict. By his second season, however, he had loosened up some. Players no longer practiced in pads on Fridays. Monday practices also were lighter, used for weightlifting and film watching. "He's not Mr. High Strung anymore," defensive tackle Don Davey said. "We're looser now, and it's a big reason we're winning."

these guys?' But I don't think that will happen anymore."

On January 12, 1997, the Jaguars faced the Patriots in the AFC Championship Game. The Patriots were coached by Coughlin's mentor, Bill Parcells. Coughlin was stung by the 20–6 loss, but he knew his team's future looked bright.

Jacksonville got a scare before the next season even began when Brunell injured his knee in the preseason. But Brunell was back by the third game of the regular season. The Jaguars

and Steelers both finished the season 11–5, but Pittsburgh captured the AFC Central Division title by a tiebreaker. Jacksonville was a wild card. In the first round, it went to Denver for a rematch of the previous season's historic playoff game. This time, the Broncos won easily, 42–17. Denver and John Elway would go on to win the Super Bowl.

"It was a monkey we had to get off our back," Broncos linebacker Bill Romanowski said about beating the Jaguars. "I thought about it [the loss the previous season] the whole game."

The defeat was disappointing, but Jacksonville had played another strong season. The Jaguars proved that their success the previous year was no fluke. But could they continue it?

Yes, they could. Jacksonville, with Coughlin guiding the way, had put together one of the NFL's most talented rosters, especially on offense. On April 18, 1998, Jacksonville added another piece to the puzzle. It drafted running back Fred Taylor with the number nine overall pick in the NFL Draft. Taylor was a Florida native and a former star at the University of Florida. He was a natural fit with the Jaguars.

WHAT AN ENDING!

Quarterback Mark Brunell's first game back from his knee injury in 1997 was Jacksonville's Monday Night Football home debut. It was Week 3 against Pittsburgh. Brunell threw for 306 yards, but the game was not decided until the last play. Clyde Simmons blocked a 40-yard field-goal try and Chris Hudson returned the ball 58 yards for a touchdown. The Jaguars won 30–21.

FRED TAYLOR BREAKS A TACKLE IN A 1999 GAME AGAINST THE CINCINNATI BENGALS. TAYLOR PLAYED IN JACKSONVILLE FOR 11 SEASONS.

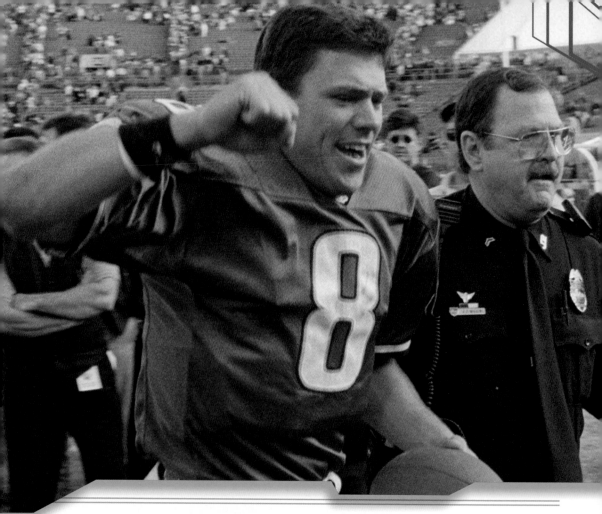

MARK BRUNELL CELEBRATES AFTER BEATING THE NEW ENGLAND PATRIOTS IN A PLAYOFF GAME AFTER THE 1998 SEASON.

The Jaguars got off to a 5–0 start in 1998. One highlight was a 28–21 win over the visiting Dolphins on October 12 on *Monday Night Football*. Taylor ran for a 77-yard touchdown. For his rookie season, he would rush for 1,223 yards and 14 touchdowns.

Brunell injured his ankle and missed the final three games of the regular season. But Jacksonville still finished 11–5 and easily won the AFC Central, its first division title. Brunell was back for the first round of the playoffs. The Jaguars, playing in their first home playoff game ever, beat the Patriots 25–10. Next up were the AFC East champion New York Jets.

Parcells coached the Jets. He had left the Patriots after the 1996 season. Now he and his team were standing in the way of Coughlin and the Jaguars again. The game was in chilly New York, and the Jets won 34–24. Brunell, playing on a left ankle that was still sore, struggled. He threw three interceptions. Coughlin was disappointed that the Jaguars turned the ball over four times.

Jacksonville's season had ended for a third straight year in the playoffs. No NFL expansion team had ever made the playoffs in three of its first four seasons. Coughlin was not satisfied with that accomplishment, however. He went back to work and planned some more.

DROPPED OPPORTUNITY

A "foolish mistake" happened in the second quarter of the Jaguars' 34–24 playoff loss to the Jets on January 10, 1999. Jacksonville safety Chris Hudson picked up a fumble by New York's Curtis Martin inside the Jaguars' 20-yard line. Then he started running down the field. The only player who had a chance to tackle Hudson was New York's slow-footed quarterback, Vinny Testaverde.

For some reason, Hudson decided to try to lateral the ball to teammate Dave Thomas. The ball came loose, and Jets wide receiver Keyshawn Johnson recovered it. "People were trying to make plays in a playoff game," Coughlin said. "Just a foolish mistake."

Jacksonville went 11–5 during the 1998 season. The Jaguars had defeated the New England Patriots 25–10 in the first round of the playoffs.

CHAPTER 4

BOOM, THEN BUST

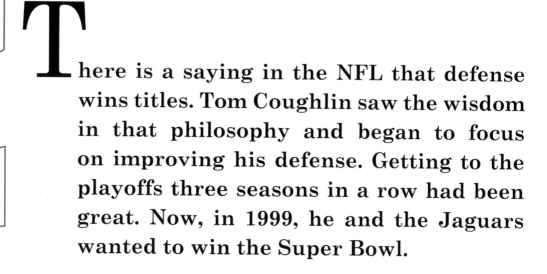

T here is a saying in the NFL that defense wins titles. Tom Coughlin saw the wisdom in that philosophy and began to focus on improving his defense. Getting to the playoffs three seasons in a row had been great. Now, in 1999, he and the Jaguars wanted to win the Super Bowl.

In the Jaguars' 34–24 loss to the Jets in the 1998 playoffs, New York's Vinny Testaverde had thrown for 284 yards and Curtis Martin ran for 124. "You can't beat anybody with a defense like that," Coughlin said. "A game like that makes you think you might need to improve your defense."

Coughlin's first step toward doing that was to hire Dom Capers as defensive coordinator. Capers had been Carolina's head coach from 1995 through the 1998 season. He was known as an expert on defense. Continuing with the defense theme, Jacksonville used its first-round pick, twenty-sixth overall, in the

JAGUARS CORNERBACK FERNANDO BRYANT PICKS OFF A PASS AGAINST THE KANSAS CITY CHIEFS. THE JAGUARS PUT MORE EMPHASIS ON DEFENSE IN 1999.

1999 NFL Draft on cornerback Fernando Bryant. The team also signed free agents Gary Walker (defensive tackle) and Carnell Lake (safety).

With a new emphasis on defense, Jacksonville appeared to have few weaknesses. More motivated than ever before, the Jaguars enjoyed their finest season in team history in 1999. The Jaguars went an NFL-best 14–2 and won 11 straight games at one point. Their only losses were to the Titans. They lost 20–19 in Jacksonville in Week 3 and 41–14 in Tennessee in Week 6.

Was there anything these Jaguars could not do? Jimmy Smith had 116 catches for 1,636 yards. James Stewart and Fred Taylor teamed to rush for 19 touchdowns and more than 1,600 yards. The defense gave up an NFL-low 217 points. Jacksonville earned the number one seed and a bye in the first round of the playoffs.

The unlucky second-round opponent was the Miami Dolphins. They never had a chance. The host Jaguars won 62–7 on January 15, 2000. The game was legendary Miami quarterback Dan Marino's last in a 17-season career. It also was Jimmy Johnson's final game as Dolphins coach. Taylor ran 90 yards for a touchdown in the first quarter, an NFL playoff record. Mark Brunell and backup quarterback Jay Fiedler both threw for

MAKING THEIR POINTS

The Jaguars' 62–7 win over the Dolphins in the 1999 playoffs was one of the most lopsided games in playoff history. The 62 points and 55-point margin of victory both placed second in NFL playoff history. "It would have even been a bad game on PlayStation," Miami wide receiver Oronde Gadsden said. Only the Bears' 73–0 win over the Redskins in the 1940 NFL Championship Game was more lopsided.

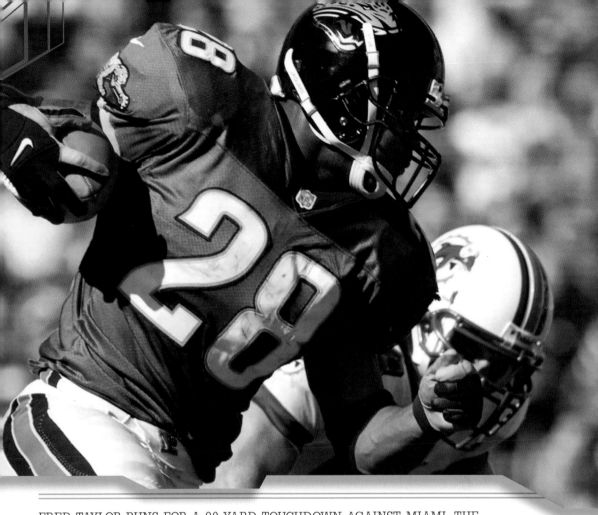

FRED TAYLOR RUNS FOR A 90-YARD TOUCHDOWN AGAINST MIAMI. THE JAGUARS BEAT THE DOLPHINS 62–7 IN THE 1999 SEASON PLAYOFF GAME.

two touchdowns. Smith had two touchdown catches. "It was a glorious day for football," Coughlin said.

It seemed as if nothing could stop Jacksonville from reaching its first Super Bowl. Unfortunately for the Jaguars, they had to face the Titans in the AFC Championship Game. Tennessee had gone 13–3 and finished second to Jacksonville in the AFC Central.

Jacksonville led 14–10 at halftime of the title game on January 23, 2000. However, visiting Tennessee scored 23 unanswered points in the second half and won 33–14 to clinch the team's first Super Bowl berth. Titans quarterback Steve McNair passed for just 112 yards, but he ran for 91 yards and two touchdowns. Brunell threw for a score but had two interceptions and lost a fumble. In a sloppy game, the Jaguars had six turnovers and the Titans four.

Jacksonville had gone 15–0 against the rest of the NFL during the 1999 regular season and postseason. Against the Titans, the Jaguars finished 0–3. "For whatever reason, we didn't play as well as we anticipated we would," Coughlin said. "It's a bitter pill to swallow."

The loss would mark the end of an era for Jacksonville. The expansion team that had done so well putting together a talented group of players would not be able to keep all of them over the next few seasons. This was because of their financial problems related to the NFL salary cap.

The NFL started using a salary cap in 1994. Under this system, the amount of money a team could spend on player salaries was limited. The Jaguars had unwisely given expensive contracts to several players during the previous several years. To stay within the salary-cap rules, they now had to start letting go of many star players. The team started playing more poorly as a result.

IT'S A WONDERFUL LIFE

One of the players whom the Jaguars could not afford to keep was running back James Stewart. In 1999, Stewart, playing part-time, ran for 931 yards and 13 touchdowns. In February 2000, he signed a five-year, $25-million contract to become the Detroit Lions' primary running back.

LINEBACKER HARDY NICKERSON WAS ONE OF MANY STAR PLAYERS JACKSONVILLE HAD TO RELEASE AROUND THE 2000–2002 SEASONS.

Injuries also affected the Jaguars. Offensive tackle Leon Searcy hurt a knee before the 2000 season and never played again in the NFL. Lake missed all of 2000 with an ailing foot. Jacksonville went 7–9 in 2000 and missed the playoffs for the first time since 1995.

The next two seasons, 2001 and 2002, were also frustrating. The Jaguars ran into more salary problems. As a result, they released veterans such as

Keenan McCardell, Lake, and linebacker Hardy Nickerson. They even made Tony Boselli, one of the most popular players in team history, available in the 2002 Expansion Draft. The NFL's newest team, the Houston Texans, chose Boselli with the first pick, though he never played for them because of injuries.

Jacksonville went 6–10 in both 2001 and 2002. The team was able to add some talented players through the NFL Draft, such as defensive tackles Marcus Stroud and John Henderson.

J. Wayne Weaver, the Jaguars' owner, decided that it was time to rebuild the team. On December 30, 2002, he fired Coughlin, who had been the Jaguars' only head coach. Weaver said it was a very tough decision, but he believed that the team needed to "move in a new direction."

Coughlin had gone 72–64, including 4–4 in the playoffs, with Jacksonville. He later would become the New York Giants' coach and lead them to the 2007 Super Bowl title.

SAYING GOOD-BYE

After Tom Coughlin was fired as coach of the Jaguars, he took out a full-page ad in the Florida Times-Union newspaper. He thanked the city of Jacksonville for "eight great seasons."

The Jaguars have not matched the success they experienced under Coughlin. They have kept trying, though, under the man who replaced him.

DEFENSIVE TACKLE MARCUS STROUD WAS ONE OF THE FEW BRIGHT SPOTS FOR JACKSONVILLE DURING THE EARLY 2000s.

CHAPTER 5

NEW COACH IN TOWN

The hiring of Jacksonville's second head coach was a big deal. Tom Coughlin had been with the Jaguars almost from the first day that they had been in the NFL.

Who would J. Wayne Weaver choose as Coughlin's replacement? He picked someone who was very different from Coughlin. On January 16, 2003, the team hired Jack Del Rio as the next head coach.

Del Rio had been Carolina's defensive coordinator in 2002. In his one year with the Panthers, their defense improved in yards allowed. They went from thirty-first—which was last in the NFL—to second.

When the Jaguars hired him, Del Rio was 39 years old—young for an NFL head coach. Del Rio had played 11 seasons as a linebacker in the NFL. Despite being a large, strong man, Del Rio was considered a "players' coach." He rarely screamed at his players, unlike Coughlin.

BYRON LEFTWICH WAS SEEN AS THE REPLACEMENT FOR MARK BRUNELL AT QUARTERBACK. THE JAGUARS SELECTED HIM IN THE 2003 DRAFT.

The Jaguars continued to rebuild over the next several months. In 2003, the team hired Ravens executive James Harris to make roster decisions. Then, on April 26, Jacksonville took Byron Leftwich, who had been a star at Marshall University, with the seventh pick in the NFL Draft. He was viewed as the quarterback who would replace Mark Brunell in the future.

That future arrived quickly. Brunell injured his throwing elbow early in the 2003 season and was out for the year. Leftwich passed for 14 touchdowns in 13 starts. He got help from Fred Taylor, who set a career high with 1,572 rushing yards. Jacksonville, though, finished only 5–11. The Jaguars still had a ways to go.

In March 2004, Jacksonville traded Brunell to the Washington Redskins. More responsibility was put on the 6-foot-5, 250-pound Leftwich's broad shoulders.

He handled it just fine. In the first game of the 2004 regular season, he threw a 7-yard touchdown pass to rookie Ernest Wilford on the game's final play to give Jacksonville a 13–10 win at Buffalo. The Jaguars finished 9–7 and barely missed making the playoffs.

JACK DEL RIO, *RIGHT*, IS KNOWN AS A PLAYERS' COACH.

"Clearly he has some of the 'it' intangibles that make a great quarterback," Del Rio said later in the season, after Leftwich had led another fourth-quarter comeback.

Jacksonville headed into the 2005 season with plenty of optimism. The Jaguars' defense had become very strong, especially in the middle of the defensive line with Marcus Stroud and John Henderson. Leftwich injured an ankle in Week 12 at Arizona, but David Garrard stepped in and led Jacksonville to four wins in the final five regular-season games. The Jaguars went 12–4.

Leftwich returned against New England in the wild-card round of the playoffs. But he was rusty, and it showed. The Patriots won 28–3.

The Jaguars had made their first playoff appearance since the 1999 season. But they knew that they would need to improve their offense. They selected Maurice Drew, who later went by Maurice Jones-Drew, with their second-round pick in the 2006 NFL Draft. However, on May 11, 2006, they lost a key offensive player when Jimmy Smith announced his retirement.

Jacksonville still went into the 2006 season with high hopes. However, Leftwich and several other players suffered season-ending injuries. Jones-Drew was a bright spot. He averaged an AFC-best 5.7 yard per carry and rushed for 13 touchdowns.

On August 31, 2007, the Jaguars surprised many people when they released Leftwich and announced that they were going with Garrard as their starting quarterback. The move worked. Garrard went 9–3 in the 12 games he started. He missed the other four with injuries. Jacksonville finished 11–5. Taylor ran for 1,202 yards, and Jones-Drew had 768. Taylor made his first Pro Bowl.

Jacksonville's opponent in the wild-card round of the 2007 playoffs was division rival Pittsburgh. The game lived up to its "wild" billing. That was thanks

DAVID GARRARD LINES UP AGAINST THE HOUSTON TEXANS IN A 2009
GAME. GARRARD TOOK OVER AS STARTING QUARTERBACK IN 2007.

in part to two touchdowns by Jones-Drew, one of which was running and the other receiving. An interception return for a score by Rashean Mathis also helped. Entering the fourth quarter, the visiting Jaguars led 28–10.

The Steelers, though, rallied for three touchdowns and took a 29–28 lead on Najeh Davenport's 1-yard run with 6:21 left. Garrard then made the game's

MAKING HISTORY

In 2004, the Jaguars became the first NFL team to have three black quarterbacks on a roster. The players were Byron Leftwich, David Garrard, and Quinn Gray.

MAURICE JONES-DREW FINDS A HOLE TO RUN THROUGH AGAINST THE INDIANAPOLIS COLTS IN 2009.

key play, running 32 yards on fourth-and-two to Pittsburgh's 11-yard line with 1:56 remaining. His scamper set up Josh Scobee's winning 25-yard field goal with 37 seconds left.

"Right before we went out, I pulled the guys together and said, 'Guys, you got to love it. This is what we're here for,' " Del Rio said about the winning 44-yard drive.

An even harder task awaited in the second round of the playoffs. Jacksonville had to play at New England. The Patriots were the first team in league history to finish the regular season 16–0. The Jaguars put up a fight. Garrard threw two touchdown passes, and the score was tied at 14 at halftime. Quarterback Tom Brady and the Patriots were playing too well, however. Brady went 26-for-28, setting an NFL record for completion percentage in any playoff or regular-season game at 92.9.

For the second time in three seasons, the Patriots ended the Jaguars' season. The team tried to address its weaknesses through free agency but it still struggled to a 5–11 record. After the 2008 season, the team decided to cut Fred Taylor.

Taylor had battled injuries throughout his career. Some fans called him "Fragile Fred." But when healthy, he was one of the NFL's best running backs. He finished his 11 seasons with Jacksonville with more than 11,000 rushing yards. On February 27, 2009, he signed a two-year contract with the Patriots.

Jones-Drew, now the main running back, rushed for a career-high 1,391 yards and 15 touchdowns in 2009, but Jacksonville lost its final four games to finish 7–9.

Del Rio's job status became a much-discussed topic. In January, owner Weaver said that Del Rio would stay at least another year. Del Rio had a 58–57 record, including 1–2 in the playoffs, in seven seasons as coach.

Despite having several successful seasons under Coughlin and Del Rio, the Jaguars are one of four NFL teams that have never appeared in the Super Bowl. The team's fans in Florida and elsewhere keep hoping for that sunny day to arrive.

TIMELINE

1989	The Touchdown Jacksonville! partnership is formed to lead the community effort to attract an NFL franchise.
1991	Armed with a $60 million commitment from the Jacksonville City Council to renovate the Gator Bowl, Touchdown Jacksonville! files an expansion application with the NFL.
1993	The NFL announces that Jacksonville is selected as the host city for the 30th NFL franchise.
1994	On February 21, the Jacksonville Jaguars hire Boston College coach Tom Coughlin as coach and director of football operations.
1995	The Jaguars select quarterback Steve Beuerlein in the NFL Expansion Draft in February. One day before the NFL Draft, the Jaguars trade for quarterback Mark Brunell. In the NFL Draft, Jacksonville takes Tony Boselli with the second pick.
1997	The Jaguars beat the Buffalo Bills and then the Denver Broncos in the playoffs before losing to the New England Patriots in the AFC Championship Game on January 12.
1998	The Jaguars select running back Fred Taylor with the ninth overall pick in the NFL Draft. Taylor will become Jacksonville's all-time leading rusher.
1999	Jacksonville, playing in its first home playoff game, defeats New England 25–10 on January 3. The Jaguars lose 34–24 to the host New York Jets in the second round.

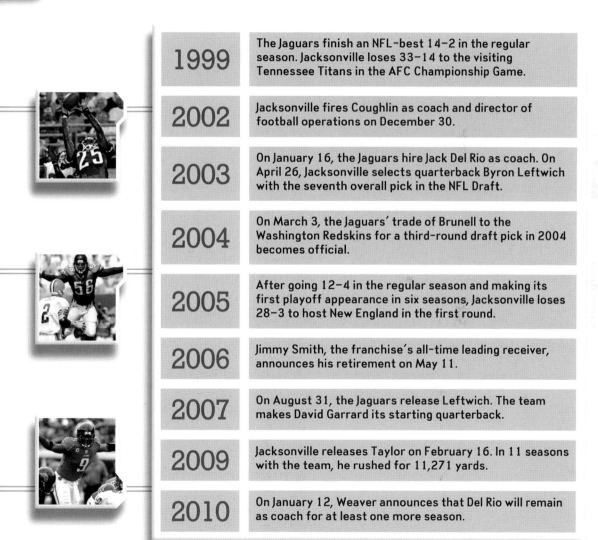

1999	The Jaguars finish an NFL-best 14–2 in the regular season. Jacksonville loses 33–14 to the visiting Tennessee Titans in the AFC Championship Game.
2002	Jacksonville fires Coughlin as coach and director of football operations on December 30.
2003	On January 16, the Jaguars hire Jack Del Rio as coach. On April 26, Jacksonville selects quarterback Byron Leftwich with the seventh overall pick in the NFL Draft.
2004	On March 3, the Jaguars' trade of Brunell to the Washington Redskins for a third-round draft pick in 2004 becomes official.
2005	After going 12–4 in the regular season and making its first playoff appearance in six seasons, Jacksonville loses 28–3 to host New England in the first round.
2006	Jimmy Smith, the franchise's all-time leading receiver, announces his retirement on May 11.
2007	On August 31, the Jaguars release Leftwich. The team makes David Garrard its starting quarterback.
2009	Jacksonville releases Taylor on February 16. In 11 seasons with the team, he rushed for 11,271 yards.
2010	On January 12, Weaver announces that Del Rio will remain as coach for at least one more season.

43

QUICK STATS

FRANCHISE HISTORY
1995–

SUPER BOWLS
None

AFC CHAMPIONSHIP GAMES
1996, 1999

DIVISION CHAMPIONSHIPS
1998, 1999

PLAYOFF APPEARANCES
1996, 1997, 1998, 1999, 2005, 2007

KEY PLAYERS
(position, seasons with team)

Tony Boselli (OT, 1995–2001)
Tony Brackens (DE, 1996–2003)
Mark Brunell (QB, 1995–2003)
Donovin Darius (S, 1998–2006)
David Garrard (QB, 2002–)
John Henderson (DT, 2002–09)
Maurice Jones–Drew
    (RB, 2006–)
Byron Leftwich (QB, 2003–06)
Rashean Mathis (CB, 2003–)
Keenan McCardell (WR, 1996–2001)
Jimmy Smith (WR, 1995–2005)
Marcus Stroud (DT, 2001–07)
Fred Taylor (RB, 1998–2008)

KEY COACHES

Tom Coughlin (1995–2002): 68–60;
    4–4 (playoffs)
Jack Del Rio (2003–): 57–55;
    1–2 (playoffs)

HOME FIELDS

Jacksonville Municipal Stadium
    (1995–)
    Also known as Alltel Stadium

*All statistics through 2009 season

QUOTES AND ANECDOTES

The Touchdown Jacksonville! business partnership was very confident that their city would get an NFL team. In fact, it had gone ahead and selected a team name, the Jaguars, in a fan contest in 1991. The Sharks, Stingrays, and even the Panthers were other finalists.

When the Jacksonville Jaguars started playing in the NFL in 1995, it meant Florida had three NFL teams: the Jaguars, the Miami Dolphins, and the Tampa Bay Buccaneers. Florida became the third state with three teams. California had the Oakland Raiders, San Diego Chargers, and San Francisco 49ers, and New York had the Buffalo Bills, New York Giants, and New York Jets. California had once had four teams, but the Rams moved to St. Louis from Los Angeles before the 1995 season.

Jacksonville fans were thrilled by their team's stunning 30–27 upset of the Denver Broncos in the second round of the 1996 playoffs. To welcome their heroes home, 40,000 Jaguars fans waited at the Jacksonville airport until 1:30 in the morning.

"Tom is one of the best two or three coaches I've ever been around. Because he's fearless—fearless. He's not afraid of anything."—Coach Bill Parcells on Jaguars coach Tom Coughlin before Parcells' New England Patriots defeated Jacksonville 20–6 in the 1996 AFC Championship Game

In 1998, Jacksonville-area McDonald's restaurants offered the "Boselli Burger" in honor of popular Jaguars offensive lineman Tony Boselli. The burger featured three hamburger patties with lettuce and tomatoes.

45

GLOSSARY

blitz

To charge directly and immediately at the passer.

contend

To compete.

contract

A binding agreement about, for example, years of commitment by a football player in exchange for a given salary.

discipline

Activity, exercise, or a regimen that develops or improves a skill; training.

draft

A system used by professional sports leagues to select new players in order to spread incoming talent among all teams.

expansion

In sports, to add a franchise or franchises to a league.

franchise

An entire sports organization including players, coaches, and staff.

lateral

To pass the ball sideways or backward.

legend

A person who achieves fame.

lopsided

Uneven; unequal.

mentor

A wise and trusted counselor or teacher.

nimble

Quick and light in movement; able to move with ease.

rookie

A first-year professional athlete.

venue

The scene or setting in which something takes place.

FOR MORE INFORMATION

Further Reading

Babula, Francis R. *Jacksonville Jaguars Record and Fact Book 1995–2002: A Fan's Guide.* Pittsburgh, PA: RoseDog Books, 2004.

MacCambridge, Michael. *America's Game: The Epic Story of how Pro Football Captured a Nation.* New York: Random House, 2004.

Sports Illustrated. *The Football Book Expanded Edition.* New York: Sports Illustrated Books, 2009.

Web Links

To learn more about the Jacksonville Jaguars, visit ABDO Publishing Company online at **www.abdopublishing.com**. Web sites about the Jaguars are featured on our Book Links page. These links are routinely monitored and updated to provide the most current information available.

Places to Visit

Jacksonville Municipal Stadium
1 Stadium Place
Jacksonville, FL 32202
904-633-6100
http://www.jaguars.com/stadium/
The Jacksonville Jaguars' home stadium.

Pro Football Hall of Fame
2121 George Halas Dr., NW
Canton, OH 44708
330-456-8207
www.profootballhof.com
This hall of fame and museum highlights the greatest players and moments in the history of the National Football League.

INDEX

About the Author

Matt Tustison specializes in editing and writing sports content at Red Line Editorial, Inc., in Burnsville, Minnesota. He previously worked as a sports copy editor at the *Baltimore Sun* and the *St. Paul Pioneer Press*, and he also has served as a freelance sports reporter for the Associated Press in Minneapolis. He graduated summa cum laude with a degree in Print Journalism from the University of St. Thomas in 2001 in his native St. Paul.